D1543246

mi casa

an introduction to commonly used Spanish words and
phrases around the home, with 500 lively photographs

JEANINE BECK

ARMADILLO

Contents

Learning Spanish

Introduce your child to Spanish from an early age by combining everyday words and phrases with lively photographs of daily activities in and around the home. Your child will enjoy learning Spanish. Let them look at the pictures and read and remember the Spanish words and phrases that accompany them. Encourage them to say the words aloud.

A NEW LANGUAGE

There is a growing need today for everyone to speak a second language. All children should have the chance to access a new language. Research shows children aged 2–8 are most receptive to linguistic learning. The younger the child, the easier it is to learn. The Spanish used in Spain differs from that spoken in Latin America and the United States in pronunciation and some vocabulary. The most noticeable difference in European Spanish pronunciation is the 'th' sound as in "cena" (theh-na) or "zapato" (tha-pat-oh). This is pronounced in America as 's' – "seh-na", " sa-pat-oh".

LEARNING TOGETHER

Children can enjoy using their Spanish all around your home. Encourage them to look at the furniture, toys and objects in each room and say the Spanish words aloud. They can use their new Spanish vocabulary to talk to their pets and when they are playing with their friends or helping you in the kitchen. You may have some Spanish-speaking friends who can talk to your children. All this will give your children a brilliant head start when they begin formal Spanish lessons at school.

LEARNING WITH PICTURES

Children respond very well to photographs and will enjoy finding pictures of things they know. Help them say and learn the Spanish words for these pictures of pets, toys and household objects around them. They can use Spanish to count things or to tell you what the children are doing. They will find out the names of all the rooms in their home. Let them take you round the house and use Spanish words to describe the things you can see.

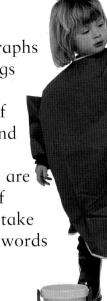

 ## IT'S FUN TO LEARN

Make learning fun by using the vocabulary on an everyday basis. Children need to demonstrate what they have learnt by playing games. You could play 'I-Spy' by choosing an object you can see and then making the sound that the word begins. Ask your child to guess what Spanish word you are thinking of and say the word aloud. The book covers such important themes as counting, opposites, clothes, food and much more. Bright and informative photographs will help the children build up their knowledge of commonly used Spanish words and phrases in a fun way. This will give them the confidence to speak Spanish.

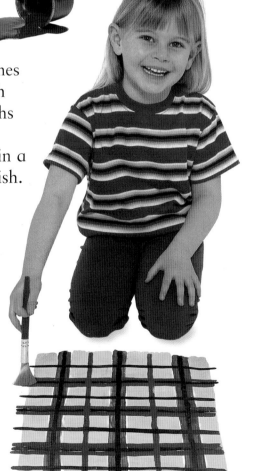

 ## HOW THE BOOK IS STRUCTURED

The key words on each page are highlighted and translated in vocabulary panels. Sentences on each page appear in both Spanish and English to help your child understand. At the end of every section is a question-and-answer game with a puzzle for you to do together and give the child a real sense of achievement. The dictionary lists all the key words and explains how they should be pronounced. Reward certificates at the end of the book test your child's knowledge of Spanish and develop confidence and self-esteem.

Mi casa

My home is special. Your home is special, too. Look at the pictures and say the words in Spanish aloud. Then use your Spanish to take your friends and family on a guided tour of your home.

La cocina

The kitchen is a fun place to work. Everyone can help to get meals ready and then tidy up.

Nos gusta preparar pasteles.
We like making cakes.

el rodillo

el bol

el molde para pastas

los huevos

	las cucharas de madera	el molde para pastas	los huevos	el rodillo
Say it with me	wooden spoons	cake pan	eggs	rolling pin

8

¡Qué sucio! ¿Quién lo limpiará?
What a mess! Who will clean it up?

María limpia el suelo.
María is washing the floor.

David

el lavavajillas

María

la mopa

el trapo
de cocina

David seca la vajilla.
David dries the dishes.

el cubo

el bol	el trapo de cocina	el lavavajillas	la mopa	el cubo
bowl	dish towel	washing-up liquid	mop	bucket

El salón

The sitting room is a family room. You can read or play games or talk or watch television.

Quiero leer.
I want to read.

el gatito

el cojín muy grande

la pelota

Pero nosotros ¡queremos jugar!
But we want to play!

Say it with me

| los libros | el cojín muy grande | la pelota | el gatito |
| books | big cushion | ball | kitten |

Luís monta un rompecabezas.
Luís is doing a jigsaw puzzle.

Luís

Alicia construye un castillo.
Alicia is building a castle.

Alicia

los cubos

el rompecabezas

¿De qué cortinas son los cubos?
What shades are the bricks?

el rompecabezas	el cubo amarillo	el cubo verde	el cubo rojo	el cubo azul
jigsaw	yellow brick	green brick	red brick	blue brick

El comedor

The dining room is a room where everyone can sit and talk over a meal.

Pedro pone la mesa.
Pedro is laying the table.

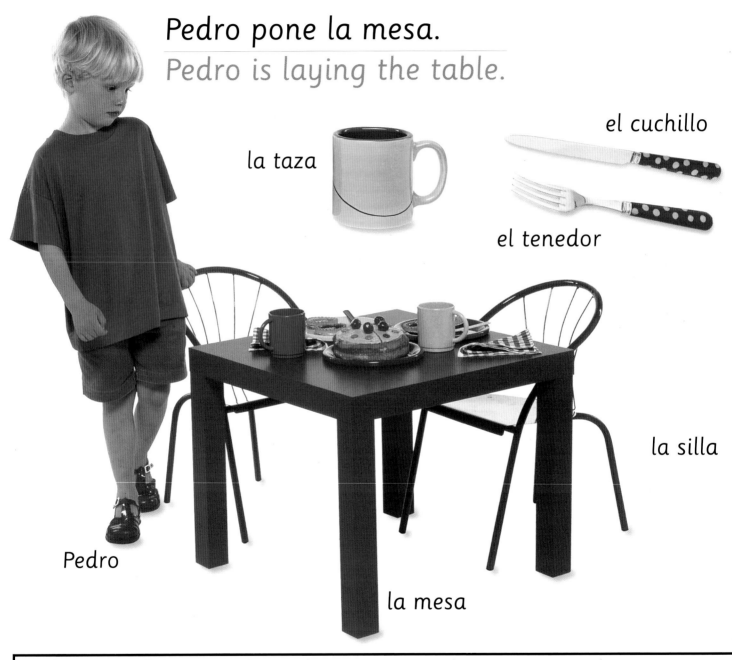

el cuchillo

la taza

el tenedor

la silla

Pedro

la mesa

12

Llevo los vasos.
I'll bring the glasses.

el plato

dos
vasos

la pizza

la bandeja

Nos gusta comer la cena.
We like eating dinner.

la mesa
table

dos vasos
two glasses

el plato
plate

la bandeja
tray

la pizza
pizza

13

El cuarto de juegos

The play room is a special place to play in. Some children keep their toys in a big toy box.

¿Qué pintas, Daniel?

What are you painting, Daniel?

Sandra

los lápices de colores

el dibujo

Daniel

el cuadro

la caja de pinturas

Pinto nuestra casa, Sandra.

I'm painting our house, Sandra.

Say it with me

el cuadro	el dibujo	la caja de pinturas
painting	drawing	paintbox

¿Te gusta bailar?
Do you like dancing?

las notas
musicales

el jugador
de música

Me gusta escuchar música.
I like listening to music.

las herramientas

Puedo reparar cosas.
I can mend things.

los lápices de colores
pencils

el jugador de música
music player

las herramientas
tools

las notas musicales
music notes

El dormitorio

The bedroom is the place to keep your clothes and all your best books and toys.

¿Quieres un cuento, Osito?
Do you want a story, Teddy?

los libros

el osito

Sí, por favor.
Yes, please.

Say it with me

los libros
books

el osito
teddy bear

la estantería
bookcase

la estanería

el cepillo

la papelera

¿Ordenas tu dormitorio?
Do you tidy your bedroom?

el cojín

los juguetes

el cepillo	la papelera	los juguetes	el cojín
carpet sweeper	bin	toys	cushion

El cuarto de baño

The bathroom is full of steam and soap and hot water. A bath gets you clean at the end of the day.

¿Quieres tomar un baño?
Would you like a bath?

el gel
de baño

el jabón

No, gracias.
No, thank you.

la bañera

la toalla

la esponja

Say it with me

el jabón	el gel de baño	la esponja	la bañera
soap	bubble bath	sponge	bath

Me cepillo los dientes.
I am brushing my teeth.

Yo también.
Me too.

la pasta
de dientes

el cepillo
de dientes

el pato

el barquito

¿Cuántos patos hay?
How many ducks are there?

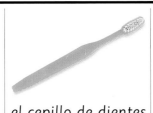

el barquito	la toalla	el cepillo de dientes	la pasta de dientes	el pato
boat	towel	toothbrush	toothpaste	duck

El jardín

The garden is really hot today! Let's go out to plant flowers, play ball and paddle.

Estamos en el jardín.
We are in the garden.

las flores

la regadera

la jardinera

¿Cuántas niñas hay?
How many girls are there?

Say it with me

| la jardinera | las flores | la regadera |
| plant pot | flowers | watering can |

¿Quién atrapará la pelota?
Who will catch the ball?

la niña
pequeña

el niño

la niña
grande

la piscina hinchable

¡El agua está fría!
The water is cold!

la niña grande
big girl

la niña pequeña
little girl

el niño
boy

la piscina hinchable
paddling pool

21

El garaje

The garage is the place to keep cars and bicycles and scooters. Sonia keeps her tricycle in the garage.

Sonia tiene un triciclo.
Sonia has a tricycle.

Sonia

el osito

el triciclo

¡Sujétate bien, Osito!
Hold on, Teddy!

el monopatín

Say it with me

el monopatín	el osito	el triciclo	el coche
scooter	teddy bear	tricycle	car

22

Lavamos el coche.
We are washing the car.

la rueda

el coche

la bata

el cubo

la esponja

el detergente

¿Puedo ayudar?
Can I help?

el detergente	la esponja	la rueda	el cubo	la bata
detergent	sponge	wheel	bucket	apron

Puzzle time

Now you know about the rooms in your home.
Write the missing words in the sentences and
fill in the crossword with the words in Spanish.

1 Las flores crecen en el jardín.

The flowers are growing in the _ _ _ _ _ _ _.

2 Los patos nadan en el baño.

The ducks swim in the _ _ _ _ _.

3 Guardo mi triciclo en el garaje.

I keep my tricycle in the _ _ _ _ _ _ _.

4 Leo un libro en el salón.

I am reading in the _____ _____.

5 Comemos la cena en el comedor.

We are eating _____ in the dining room.

Now try my crossword!

	1		2	
3				

6 Limpio el suelo de la cocina.

I am washing the _____ floor.

Un día
en casa

A day at home gives you a chance to talk to your family and pets in Spanish. Look at these exciting photographs of the things you do every day – and say the words aloud. You can speak Spanish!

Levantarse

Getting up in the morning is easy for some people. Other people need an alarm clock.

Buenos días, Osito.
Good morning, Teddy.

Miranda

el reloj

Buenos días, Miranda.
Good morning, Miranda.

la cama

la manta

los zapatos

Say it with me

la cama	la manta	el reloj	el suéter
bed	blanket	clock	sweater

¡Mira! Estoy vestida.
Look! I'm dressed.

la camisa

el suéter

la falda

la alineada

los calcetines

Me pongo el suéter.
I am putting on my sweater.

los zapatos
shoes

la camisa
shirt

la falda
skirt

los calcetines
socks

la alineada
dress

Desayunar

Eating breakfast is a good way to start the morning. What do you want to eat today?

¿Qué hay para desayunar?
What's for breakfast?

las tostadas

el huevo frito

el panecillo

la mantequilla

Say it with me

la mantequilla	el panecillo	el huevo frito	las tostadas
butter	bread roll	fried egg	toast

la miel

la leche

el zumo
de man-
zana

la fruta

Como los cereales.
I am eating cereal.

los cereales

la miel
honey

la leche
milk

el zumo de manzana
apple juice

la fruta
fruit

los cereales
cereal

Jugar con mis amigos

Playing with friends is fun! They can visit you at home, and you can play lots of games.

Ven a nuestra merienda.
Come to our tea party.

la tetera

¿Puedes contar las tazas?
Can you count the cups?

los ositos

Say it with me

la cuchara	el plato	la tetera	la taza
spoon	plate	teapot	cup

¿Dónde está todo el mundo?
Where is everyone?

la maleta

Estoy en la maleta.
I am in the suitcase.

la caja de sorpresas

la ven-
tana

Estoy en la caja.
I am in the box.

la casa

la puerta

Estamos en la casa.
We are in the house.

la maleta
suitcase

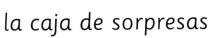

la ventana
window

la casa
house

la puerta
door

la caja de sorpresas
jack in the box

Un paseo en el parque

A walk in the park gets you out of the house.
You can walk the dog and feed the ducks.

¿Vamos al parque?

Shall we go to the park?

Magdalena

el perro

la ardilla

el pato

Sí, por favor, Magdalena.

Yes, please, Magdalena.

la correa

Say it with me

el perro
dog

la correa
leash

la ardilla
squirrel

Queremos dar de comer a los patos.
We want to feed the ducks.

la bolsa

las botas

Doy de comer a los patos.
I am feeding the ducks.

el patito

la bolsa bag	**las botas** boots	**el pato** duck	**el patito** duckling

La hora de cenar

Dinnertime is the main meal of the day.
What do you like eating best?

¿Qué vamos a cenar hoy?
What shall we eat today?

la pasta

la sopa del
tomate

la leche

Say it with me

	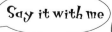		
la pasta	la leche	la sopa del tomate	la fruta
pasta	milk	tomato soup	fruit

36

la fruta

el pollo

la salchicha

el queso

las galletas
de perro

las verduras

Victor tiene hambre.
Victor is hungry.

el pollo
chicken

el queso
cheese

la salchicha
sausage

las verduras
vegetables

las galletas de perro
dog biscuits

La hora de dormir

Bedtime is sleepy time. You can read a book in bed or listen to a story or just go to sleep.

¡No tengo sueño!
I'm not sleepy!

el dragón

la cama

el perro

¿Cuántos animales hay en la cama?
How many animals are in the bed?

¡Buenas noches!
Good night!

el gato

Say it with me

el dragón
dragon

la cama
bed

el perro
dog

¿Qué te pones para dormir?
What do you wear at bedtime?

el camisón

el pijama

¿Dónde están mis zapatillas?
Where are my slippers?

las zapatillas

el gato
cat

el pijama
pyjamas

el camisón
nightdress

las zapatillas
slippers

Puzzle time

Some words are missing from the sentences. Can you fill them in and complete the Lost Letters puzzle with their Spanish names?

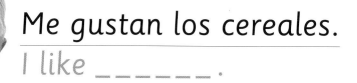

Me gustan los cereales.
I like _ _ _ _ _ _ .

El reloj marca la hora.
The _ _ _ _ _ tells the time.

Al osito le gusta la casa.
The _ _ _ _ _ likes the _ _ _ _ _ .

La niña come un bocadillo de salchicha y fruta.

The ____ eats a hot dog and _____ .

El perro es marrón.

The ___ is brown.

Try to find the lost letters

El dragón se va a la cama.

The dragon goes to ___ .

	c e r e a l e s
	r _ l _ j
	o _ _ _ o
	_ a _ a
	n _ ñ _
	f r _ _ _
	_ _ r r _
	_ a _ a

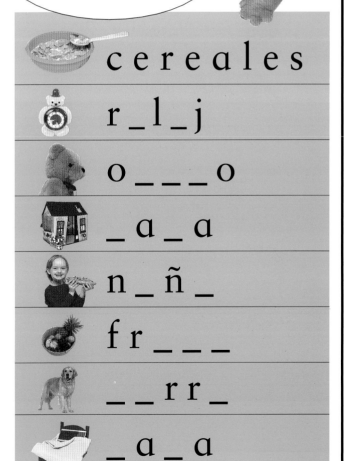

41

La hora de jugar

Playtime is the happiest part of the day, and you can learn Spanish at the same time! You can speak Spanish while you are playing games or having fun with your friends.

Pintar

Painting is a messy thing to do! You can paint with a paintbrush or your hands or feet.

Mis pantalones tienen cuadros.
My trousers have checks.

los pinceles

la caja
de pinturas

Me gusta pintar cuadros.
I like painting checks.

44

¿Te gusta mi cuadro?
Do you like my painting?

negro

blanco

azul

amarillo

rojo

verde

naranja

¡Pinto con mis pies!
I'm painting with my feet!

rojo	amarillo	azul	naranja	verde
red	yellow	blue	orange	green

45

Tocar música

Making music is great fun. Some people play instruments, others like to dance.

la araña

¿Bailas?

Are you dancing?

el gatito

la bailarina

No. Estoy cazando una araña.

No. I'm catching a spider.

Say it with me

la bailarina	el gatito	la araña	la guitarra
dancer	kitten	spider	guitar

Toco la guitarra.
I play the guitar.

la flauta

el tambor

la guitarra

la pandereta

el xilófono

la trompeta

¿Sabes tocar el xilófono?
Can you play the xylophone?

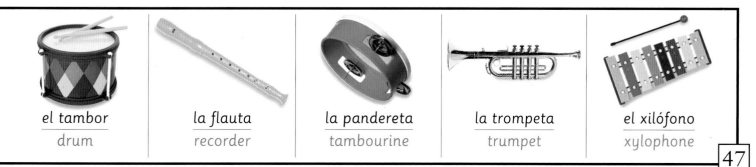

el tambor	la flauta	la pandereta	la trompeta	el xilófono
drum	recorder	tambourine	trumpet	xylophone

Disfrazarse

Dressing up is an adventure. You can be a pretty fairy or a magic wizard.

Tengo una varita mágica.
I have a wand.

el mago

la varita mágica

el sombrero

el hada

Soy un mago.
I'm a wizard.

Say it with me

el hada	la varita mágica	el sombrero	el mago
fairy	wand	hat	wizard

¿Puedes ver mi loro?
Can you see my parrot?

el vaquero

el payaso

el pirata

el loro

¿Dónde está mi placa?
Where's my badge?

Soy un payaso.
I'm a clown.

la placa

el pirata
pirate

el loro
parrot

el payaso
clown

el vaquero
cowboy

la placa
badge

De compras

Playing shopping is fun. Count the food before you put it in your basket.

<u>¿Qué voy a comprar?</u>
What shall I buy?

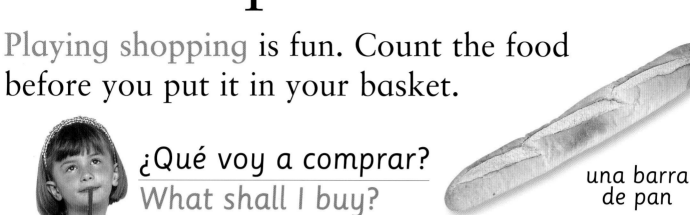

una barra
de pan

dos pasteles

tres helados

la cesta

cuatro plátanos

la cesta	una barra de pan	dos pasteles	tres helados	cuatro plátanos
basket	one bread loaf	two cakes	three ice creams	four bananas

cinco bombones

seis manzanas

siete cebollas

ocho cerezas

nueve tomates

diez latas

Estoy de compras.

I am shopping.

cinco bombones

five chocolates

seis manzanas

six apples

siete cebollas

seven onions

ocho cerezas

eight cherries

nueve tomates

nine tomatoes

diez latas

ten cans

51

Bajo la lluvia

Getting wet is fantastic fun.
You can splash in all the puddles.

la lluvia

Me caí en el charco.
I fell in the puddle.

las botas

el charco

Me gusta jugar en la lluvia.
I like playing in the rain.

Say it with me

el charco	las botas	la lluvia
puddle	boots	rain

Nos gusta pescar bajo la lluvia.
We like fishing in the rain.

la capucha

la caña de pescar

el pez

el impermeable

¡Hemos capturado dos peces!
We've caught two fish!

el impermeable
raincoat

la capucha
rainhat

la caña de pescar
fishing rod

el pez
fish

Los juegos

Playing games is fun. You can play with your friends and get some exercise too!

la pelota

¿Puedes lanzar una pelota?
Can you throw a ball?

el casco

lanzar

la bicicleta

¿Quién gana la carrera?
Who is winning the race?

Say it with me

la pelota	lanzar	el casco	la bicicleta
ball	throw	helmet	bicycle

Nos gusta practicar deporte.
We like sport.

los patines

el balon-cesto

el monopatín

los bolos

¿Quién está arriba?
Who is high?

saltar

¿Quién está abajo?
Who is low?

el baloncesto
basketball

los patines
roller skates

el monopatín
skateboard

los bolos
skittles

saltar
jump

Puzzle time

Can you count from one to six in Spanish?
The Spanish numbers are in the Word Square.

Un niño lanza una pelota.
___ boy throwing a ball.

Dos niños pescan.
___ boys fishing.

Tres instrumentos musicales.
_____ musical instruments.

Cuatro niños saltan.

_ _ _ _ children jumping.

El payaso hace
malabarismos con cinco pelotas.

The clown is juggling _ _ _ _ balls.

Find the Spanish
numbers in my
word square

Seis huellas.

_ _ _ footprints.

a	c	u	a	t	r	o
u	h	a	b	r	l	o
n	o	t	c	e	a	q
o	u	r	c	s	n	q
o	n	c	i	n	c	o
d	o	s	x	a	n	o
c	h	i	s	e	i	s

How Spanish works

Encourage your child to enjoy learning Spanish and go further in the language. You may find these basic tips on how the Spanish language works helpful. Check out the dictionary, since it lists all the key words in the book and will help you and your child pronounce the words correctly.

MASCULINE/FEMININE

All nouns are masculine (el, un) or feminine (la, una). 'Los' or 'unos' are used in the plural for masculine nouns, 'las' or 'unas' for feminine nouns.

COMPARING THINGS

When we want to compare things in English, we say they are, for example, small, smaller or smallest. This is the pattern in Spanish:

SPANISH	ENGLISH
Es pequeño	He is small
Es más pequeño	He is smaller
Es el más pequeño	He is the smallest

ADJECTIVES

As a general rule, feminine adjectives end in 'a' (e.g. la niña pequeña) and masculine adjectives in 'o' (e.g. el niño pequeño). If the adjective does not end in 'o' or 'a' it does not change.

PERSONAL PRONOUNS

SPANISH	ENGLISH
yo	I
tú	you (singular)
usted	you (singular polite)
él or ella	he or she
nosotros	we
vosotros	you (plural)
ustedes	you (plural polite)
ellos or ellas	they

'Tú' and 'vosotros' (plural) are used for talking to people you know. 'Usted' and 'ustedes' (plural) are used when you are talking to someone you don't know and are being polite.

VERBS

Spanish verbs change their endings depending on which personal pronoun and tense are used. This book uses only the present tense but there are other tenses in Spanish including the past and the future.

Help your child find the language pattern that emerges in the endings of the verbs. There are three groups of verbs which follow a regular pattern: those ending in 'ar', 'er' and 'ir'. Point out that in the verbs given here, 'tú' either ends in '-as' or '-es' and 'usted' either in '-a' or '-e' whilst 'vosotros' ends in '-áis', '-éis' or 'ís' and 'ustedes' in '-an' or '-en'. Play a game by saying the first word aloud – 'Yo', 'Tú'. Let your child answer with the verb – 'salto', 'saltas'.

Here are three simple verbs in the present tense. Look at the ends of the words and say the Spanish out loud.

SPANISH	ENGLISH
saltar	*to jump*
Yo salto	I jump
Tú saltas	You jump
Usted salta	You jump (polite)
Él/ella salta	He/she jumps
Nosotros saltamos	We jump
Vosotros saltáis	You jump (plural)
Ustedes saltan	You jump (plural polite)
Ellos/ellas saltan	They jump

SPANISH	ENGLISH
comer	*to eat*
Yo como	I eat
Tú comes	You eat
Usted come	You eat (polite)
Él/ella come	He/she eats
Nosotros comemos	We eat
Vosotros coméis	You eat (plural)
Ustedes comen	You eat (plural polite)
Ellos/ellas comen	They eat

decir	*to say*
Yo digo	I say
Tú dices	You say
Usted dice	You say (polite)
Él/ella dice	He/she says
Nosotros decimos	We say
Vosotros decís	You say (plural)
Ustedes dicen	You say (pl. pol.)
Ellos/ellas dicen	They say

Pronunciation Key

SPANISH	SAY	EXAMPLE
a	*a*	*cama: ka-ma*
ai	*eye*	*bailarina: bye-la-ree-na*
e	*eh*	*leche: leh-cheh*
u	*oo*	*lunes: loo-nez*
ue	*weh*	*puerta: pwehr-ta*
b	*b*	*bolsa: bol-sa*
v	*b*	*vaso: ba-soh*
c	*k*	*casa: ka-sa*
c	*th*	*cepillo: theh-pee-yoh*
h	*this is not pronounced*	*hada: ada*
g	*g*	*gato: ga-toh*
g	*h*	*mágica: ma-hika*
j	*h*	*jabón: ha-bon*
gu	*g*	*juguetes: hoo-geh-tez*
ll	*y*	*ardilla: ar-dee-ya*
ñ	*ny*	*bañera: ban-yehr-a*
z	*th*	*taza: ta-tha*

El diccionario

ENGLISH	SPANISH	SAY
A		
apple	la manzana	*la man-than-a*
apple juice	el zumo de manzana	*el thoo-moh deh man-than-a*
apron	la bata	*la ba-ta*
B		
badge	la placa	*la pla-ka*
bag	la bolsa	*la bol-sa*
ball	la pelota	*la pel-oh-ta*
banana	el plátano	*el pla-ta-noh*
basket	la cesta	*la thes-ta*
basketball	el baloncesto	*el bah-lon-thes-toh*
bath	la bañera	*la ban-yehr-a*
bathroom	el cuarto de baño	*el kwar-toh deh ban-yoh*
bed	la cama	*la ka-ma*
bedroom	el dormitorio	*el dor-mee-tor-ee-oh*
bicycle	la bicicleta	*la bee-thee-kleh-ta*
bin	la papelera	*la pa-peh-lehr-a*
boat	el barquito	*el bar-keet-oh*
bookcase	la estantería	*la es-tan-tehr-ee-a*
books	los libros	*los lee-broz*
boots	las botas	*las boh-taz*
bowl	el bol	*el bol*
boy	el niño	*el nee-nyo*

Shades

ENGLISH	SPANISH	SAY
black	negro	*neh-groh*
blue	azul	*a-thool*
brown	marrón	*mar-ron*
green	verde	*behr-deh*
grey	gris	*grees*
orange	naranja	*na-ran-ha*
red	rojo	*roh-hoh*
white	blanco	*blan-koh*
yellow	amarillo	*am-ar-ee-yoh*

ENGLISH	SPANISH	SAY
bread loaf	la barra de pan	*la bar-ra deh pan*
bread roll	el panecillo	*el pan-e-thee-yoh*
breakfast	el desayuno	*el des-a-yoo-noh*
brick	el cubo	*el koo-boh*
brushes	los pinceles	*los pin-theh-lez*
bubble bath	el gel de baño	*el hel deh ban-yoh*
bucket	el cubo	*el koo-boh*
butter	la mantequilla	*la man-teh-kee-ya*
C		
cake	el pastel	*el pas-tel*
cake pan	el molde para pastas	*el mol-deh para pas-taz*
can	la lata	*la la-ta*
car	el coche	*el ko-cheh*
carpet sweeper	el cepillo	*el theh-pee-yoh*
cat	el gato	*el ga-toh*
cereal	los cereales	*los theh-reh-al-ez*
chair	la silla	*la see-ya*
cheese	el queso	*el keh-soh*
cherries	las cerezas	*las theh-reh-thaz*
chicken	el pollo	*el po-yoh*
chocolates	los bombones	*los bom-boh-nez*
clock	el reloj	*el reh-loh*
clown	el payaso	*el pa-ya-soh*
cowboy	el vaquero	*el bak-ehr-oh*
cup	la taza	*la ta-tha*
cushion	el cojín	*el ko-heen*
D		
dancer	la bailarina	*la bye-la-ree-na*
detergent	el detergente	*el deh-tehr-hen-teh*
dining room	el comedor	*el ko-meh-dohr*
dinner	la cena	*la theh-na*
dish towel	el trapo de cocina	*el tra-po deh ko-thee-na*
dog	el perro	*el per-roh*
dog biscuits	las galletas de perro	*las ga-yet-az deh per-roh*
door	la puerta	*la pwehr-ta*
dragon	el dragón	*el dra-gon*
drawing	el dibujo	*el dee-boo-hoh*
dress	la alineada	*la al-in-eh-ada*

Days of the week

ENGLISH	SPANISH	SAY
Monday	lunes	*loo-nez*
Tuesday	martes	*mar-tez*
Wednesday	miércoles	*mee-ehr-koh-lez*
Thursday	jueves	*hweh-bez*
Friday	viernes	*bee-ehr-nez*
Saturday	sábado	*sa-ba-doh*
Sunday	domingo	*do-ming-goh*

ENGLISH	SPANISH	SAY
drum	el tambor	*el tam-bohr*
duck	el pato	*el pa-toh*
duckling	el patito	*el pa-tee-toh*

E and F

eggs	los huevos	*los weh-boz*
fairy	el hada	*el ada*
fish	el pez	*el peth*
fishing rod	la caña de pescar	*la kan-ya deh pes-kar*
flowerpot	la maceta	*la ma-theh-ta*
fork	el tenedor	*el teh-neh-dohr*
fried egg	el huevo frito	*el weh-boh free-toh*
fruit	la fruta	*la froo-ta*

G and H

garage	el garaje	*el gar-a-heh*
garden	el jardín	*el har-deen*
girl	la niña	*la nee-nya*
glass	el vaso	*el ba-soh*
guitar	la guitarra	*la gee-tar-ra*
helmet	el casco	*el kas-koh*
honey	la miel	*la mee-yel*
house	la casa	*la ka-sa*

I and J

ice cream	el helado	*el eh-la-doh*

ENGLISH	SPANISH	SAY
jack in the box	la caja de sorpresas	*la ka-ha deh sor-preh-saz*
jigsaw puzzle	el rompe-cabezas	*el rom-peh-ka-beh-thaz*

K and L

kitchen	la cocina	*la koh-thee-na*
kitten	el gatito	*el ga-tee-toh*
knife	el cuchillo	*el koo-chee-yoh*
leash	la correa	*la kor-reh-a*

M, N and O

mechanical	mecánico	*meh-kan-i-koh*
milk	la leche	*la leh-cheh*
mop	la mopa	*la moh-pa*
mug	la taza	*la ta-tha*
music notes	las notas musicales	*las noh-taz moo-zik-al-ez*
music player	el jugador de música	*el hoo-ga-dohr moo-zik-ah*
nightdress	el camisón	*el ka-mees-on*
onions	las cebollas	*las theh-bo-yee-az*

Months of the year

ENGLISH	SPANISH	SAY
January	enero	*en-ehr-oh*
February	febrero	*feb-rehr-oh*
March	marzo	*mar-thoh*
April	abril	*ab-reel*
May	mayo	*ma-yoh*
June	junio	*hoo-nee-oh*
July	julio	*hoo-lee-oh*
August	agosto	*ag-ost-oh*
September	septiembre	*sep-tee-em-breh*
October	octubre	*ok-too-breh*
November	noviembre	*nob-ee-em-breh*
December	diciembre	*dith-ee-em-breh*

ENGLISH	SPANISH	SAY
P		
paddling pool	la piscina hinchable	*la pees-thee-na in-cha-bleh*
paintbox	la caja de pinturas	*la ka-ha deh peen-too-raz*
painting	el cuadro	*el kwad-roh*
parrot	el loro	*el lo-roh*
pasta	la pasta	*la pas-ta*
pencils	los lápices	*los la-pi-thez*
pirate	el pirata	*el pee-ra-ta*
pizza	la pizza	*la peet-za*
plant pot	la jardinera	*la har-dee-nehr-a*
plate	el plato	*el pla-toh*
play room	el cuarto de juegos	*el kwar-toh deh hweh-goz*
puddle	el charco	*el char-koh*
pyjamas	el pijama	*el pee-hama*
R		
rain	la lluvia	*la yoo-bee-a*
raincoat	el impermeable	*el im-pehr-meh-ableh*
rainhat	la capucha	*la ka-poo-cha*
recorder	la flauta	*la fl-aw-ta*
roller skates	los patines	*los pa-tee-nez*
S		
sausage	la salchicha	*la sal-chee-cha*
scooter	el monopatín	*el mono-pa-teen*
shirt	la camisa	*la ka-mee-sa*

Numbers

ENGLISH	SPANISH	SAY
one	uno (m.)/una (f.)	*oo-no/oo-na*
two	dos	*dos*
three	tres	*tres*
four	cuatro	*kwa-troh*
five	cinco	*thing-koh*
six	seis	*seh-ees*
seven	siete	*see-eh-teh*
eight	ocho	*och-oh*
nine	nueve	*noo-eh-beh*
ten	diez	*dee-eth*

62

ENGLISH	SPANISH	SAY
shoes	los zapatos	*los tha-pa-toz*
sitting room	el salón	*el sa-lon*
skateboard	el monopatín	*el mono-pa-teen*
skirt	la falda	*la fal-da*
skittles	los bolos	*los boh-loz*
slippers	las zapatillas	*las tha-pa-tee-yaz*
soap	el jabón	*el ha-bon*
socks	los calcetines	*los kal-theh-teen-ez*
soft toy	el peluche	*el pel-ooch-eh*
soup	la sopa	*la soh-pah*
spider	la araña	*la ar-anya*
sponge	la esponja	*la es-pong-ha*
spoon	la cuchara	*la koo-chara*
squirrel	la ardilla	*la ar-dee-ya*
suitcase	la maleta	*la ma-leh-ta*
sun	el sol	*el sol*
sweater	el suéter	*el soo-et-ehr*
T		
table	la mesa	*la meh-sa*
tambourine	la pandereta	*la pan-deh-reh-ta*
teapot	la tetera	*la teh-teh-ra*
teddy bear	el osito	*el os-ee-toh*
to jump	saltar	*sal-tar*
to throw	lanzar	*lan-thar*
toast	la tostada	*la tos-ta-da*
tools	las herramientas	*las err-a-mee-en-taz*
toothbrush	el cepillo de dientes	*el theh-pee-yoh deh dee-en-tez*
toothpaste	la pasta de dientes	*la pas-ta deh dee-en-tez*
towel	la toalla	*la toh-a-ya*
toys	los juguetes	*los hoo-geh-tez*
tray	la bandeja	*la ban-deh-ha*
trumpet	la trompeta	*la trom-peh-ta*

V, W and X

vegetables	las verduras	*las behr-doo-raz*
wand	la varita mágica	*la bar-ee-ta ma-hika*
washing-up liquid	el lavavajillas	*el la-ba-ba-hee-yaz*
watering can	la regadera	*la reh-ga-dehr-a*
wheel	la rueda	*la rweh-da*
window	la ventana	*la ben-ta-na*
wizard	el mago	*el ma-goh*
wooden spoons	las cucharas de madera	*las koo-charaz deh mahd-ehr-a*
xylophone	el xilófono	*el zee-lof-on-oh*

This is to certify that

_____

can count
from one to ten
in Spanish

Date _____

This is to certify that

_____

can name
five toys
in Spanish

Date _____

This is to certify that

_____

can name
six shades
in Spanish

Date _____

This is to certify that

_____

can name the
rooms in a house
in Spanish

Date _____

This edition is published by Armadillo, an imprint of Anness Publishing Ltd,
108 Great Russell Street, London WC1B 3NA; info@anness.com

www.armadillobooks.co.uk; www.annesspublishing.com; twitter: @Anness_Books

If you like the images in this book and would like to investigate using
them forpublishing, promotions or advertising, please visit our website
www.practicalpictures.com for more information.

A CIP catalogue record for this book is available
from the British Library.

Publisher: Joanna Lorenz
Editor: Joy Wotton
Designer: Maggi Howells
Photography: Jane Burton, John Daniels, John Freeman,
Robert Pickett, Kim Taylor, Lucy Tizard

The publishers wish to thank all the children
who appear in this book.

PUBLISHER'S NOTE
The author and publishers have made every effort to ensure that this
book is safe for its intended use, and cannot accept any legal responsibility
or liability for any harm or injury arising from misuse.

Manufacturer: Anness Publishing Ltd, 108 Great Russell Street, London WC1B 3NA, England
For Product Tracking go to: www.annesspublishing.com/tracking
Batch: 4259-23639-1127